A year of living happ

MW01119314

Use this gratitude journal to recover from divorce by reminding yourself on a daily basis why getting a divorce was the best thing that happened to you.

Embrace your newly single status,
and discover a happier, healthier self.

This journal includes space for 365 daily reflections.
Use it to rebuild your life, by writing down reasons you are grateful, thankful and happy to be divorced.

Examples of thoughts you may like to explore
in this journal:

- *Reasons I got a divorce*
- *Ways I'm happier now after I divorced*
- *Great things that have happened to me since my divorce*
- *Things I'm free to do now that I'm single*
- *Good riddance to the bad habits of my ex*
- *Ways I'm healthier (mentally and physically) after my divorce*

Important Dates and Numbers

Date of my divorce:

_____

I started this journal on:

_____

The top 3 reasons I got a divorce:

1. _____

2. _____

3. _____

All the reasons I'm happily divorced

Date: _____

_____

_____

_____

Date: _____

_____

_____

_____

Date: _____

_____

_____

_____

Date: _____

_____

_____

_____

All the reasons I'm happily divorced

Date: _____

_____

_____

_____

Date: _____

_____

_____

_____

Date: _____

_____

_____

_____

Date: _____

_____

_____

_____

All the reasons I'm happily divorced

Date: _____

_____

_____

_____

Date: _____

_____

_____

_____

Date: _____

_____

_____

_____

Date: _____

_____

_____

_____

All the reasons I'm happily divorced

Date: _____

_____

_____

_____

Date: _____

_____

_____

_____

Date: _____

_____

_____

_____

Date: _____

_____

_____

_____

All the reasons I'm happily divorced

Date: _____

_____

_____

_____

Date: _____

_____

_____

_____

Date: _____

_____

_____

_____

Date: _____

_____

_____

_____

All the reasons I'm happily divorced

Date: _____

_____

_____

_____

Date: _____

_____

_____

_____

Date: _____

_____

_____

_____

Date: _____

_____

_____

_____

All the reasons I'm happily divorced

Date: _____

_____

_____

_____

Date: _____

_____

_____

_____

Date: _____

_____

_____

_____

Date: _____

_____

_____

_____

All the reasons I'm happily divorced

Date: _____

_____

_____

_____

Date: _____

_____

_____

_____

Date: _____

_____

_____

_____

Date: _____

_____

_____

_____

All the reasons I'm happily divorced

Date: _____

_____

_____

_____

Date: _____

_____

_____

_____

Date: _____

_____

_____

_____

Date: _____

_____

_____

_____

All the reasons I'm happily divorced

Date: _____

_____

_____

_____

Date: _____

_____

_____

_____

Date: _____

_____

_____

_____

Date: _____

_____

_____

_____

All the reasons I'm happily divorced

Date: _____

_____

_____

_____

Date: _____

_____

_____

_____

Date: _____

_____

_____

_____

Date: _____

_____

_____

_____

All the reasons I'm happily divorced

Date: _____

_____

_____

_____

Date: _____

_____

_____

_____

Date: _____

_____

_____

_____

Date: _____

_____

_____

_____

All the reasons I'm happily divorced

Date: _____

_____

_____

_____

Date: _____

_____

_____

_____

Date: _____

_____

_____

_____

Date: _____

_____

_____

_____

All the reasons I'm happily divorced

Date: _____

_____

_____

_____

Date: _____

_____

_____

_____

Date: _____

_____

_____

_____

Date: _____

_____

_____

_____

All the reasons I'm happily divorced

Date: _____

_____

_____

_____

Date: _____

_____

_____

_____

Date: _____

_____

_____

_____

Date: _____

_____

_____

_____

All the reasons I'm happily divorced

Date: _____

_____
_____
_____

Date: _____

_____
_____
_____

Date: _____

_____
_____
_____

Date: _____

_____
_____
_____

All the reasons I'm happily divorced

Date: _____

_____

_____

_____

Date: _____

_____

_____

_____

Date: _____

_____

_____

_____

Date: _____

_____

_____

_____

All the reasons I'm happily divorced

Date: _____

_____

_____

_____

Date: _____

_____

_____

_____

Date: _____

_____

_____

_____

Date: _____

_____

_____

_____

All the reasons I'm happily divorced

Date: _____

_____

_____

_____

Date: _____

_____

_____

_____

Date: _____

_____

_____

_____

Date: _____

_____

_____

_____

All the reasons I'm happily divorced

Date: _____

_____

_____

_____

Date: _____

_____

_____

_____

Date: _____

_____

_____

_____

Date: _____

_____

_____

_____

All the reasons I'm happily divorced

Date: _____

_____

_____

_____

Date: _____

_____

_____

_____

Date: _____

_____

_____

_____

Date: _____

_____

_____

_____

All the reasons I'm happily divorced

Date: _____

_____

_____

_____

Date: _____

_____

_____

_____

Date: _____

_____

_____

_____

Date: _____

_____

_____

_____

All the reasons I'm happily divorced

Date: _____

_____

_____

_____

Date: _____

_____

_____

_____

Date: _____

_____

_____

_____

Date: _____

_____

_____

_____

All the reasons I'm happily divorced

Date: _____

_____

_____

_____

Date: _____

_____

_____

_____

Date: _____

_____

_____

_____

Date: _____

_____

_____

_____

All the reasons I'm happily divorced

Date: _____

_____

_____

_____

Date: _____

_____

_____

_____

Date: _____

_____

_____

_____

Date: _____

_____

_____

_____

All the reasons I'm happily divorced

Date: _____

_____

_____

_____

Date: _____

_____

_____

_____

Date: _____

_____

_____

_____

Date: _____

_____

_____

_____

All the reasons I'm happily divorced

Date: _____

_____

_____

_____

Date: _____

_____

_____

_____

Date: _____

_____

_____

_____

Date: _____

_____

_____

_____

All the reasons I'm happily divorced

Date: _____

_____

_____

_____

Date: _____

_____

_____

_____

Date: _____

_____

_____

_____

Date: _____

_____

_____

_____

All the reasons I'm happily divorced

Date: _____

_____

_____

_____

Date: _____

_____

_____

_____

Date: _____

_____

_____

_____

Date: _____

_____

_____

_____

All the reasons I'm happily divorced

Date: _____

_____

_____

_____

Date: _____

_____

_____

_____

Date: _____

_____

_____

_____

Date: _____

_____

_____

_____

All the reasons I'm happily divorced

Date: _____

_____

_____

_____

Date: _____

_____

_____

_____

Date: _____

_____

_____

_____

Date: _____

_____

_____

_____

All the reasons I'm happily divorced

Date: _____

_____

_____

_____

Date: _____

_____

_____

_____

Date: _____

_____

_____

_____

Date: _____

_____

_____

_____

All the reasons I'm happily divorced

Date: _____

_____

_____

_____

Date: _____

_____

_____

_____

Date: _____

_____

_____

_____

Date: _____

_____

_____

_____

All the reasons I'm happily divorced

Date: _____

_____

_____

_____

Date: _____

_____

_____

_____

Date: _____

_____

_____

_____

Date: _____

_____

_____

_____

All the reasons I'm happily divorced

Date: _____

_____

_____

_____

Date: _____

_____

_____

_____

Date: _____

_____

_____

_____

Date: _____

_____

_____

_____

All the reasons I'm happily divorced

Date: _____

_____

_____

_____

Date: _____

_____

_____

_____

Date: _____

_____

_____

_____

Date: _____

_____

_____

_____

All the reasons I'm happily divorced

Date: _____

_____

_____

_____

Date: _____

_____

_____

_____

Date: _____

_____

_____

_____

Date: _____

_____

_____

_____

All the reasons I'm happily divorced

Date: _____

_____

_____

_____

Date: _____

_____

_____

_____

Date: _____

_____

_____

_____

Date: _____

_____

_____

_____

All the reasons I'm happily divorced

Date: _____

_____

_____

_____

Date: _____

_____

_____

_____

Date: _____

_____

_____

_____

Date: _____

_____

_____

_____

All the reasons I'm happily divorced

Date: _____

_____

_____

_____

Date: _____

_____

_____

_____

Date: _____

_____

_____

_____

Date: _____

_____

_____

_____

All the reasons I'm happily divorced

Date: _____

_____

_____

_____

Date: _____

_____

_____

_____

Date: _____

_____

_____

_____

Date: _____

_____

_____

_____

All the reasons I'm happily divorced

Date: _____

_____

_____

_____

Date: _____

_____

_____

_____

Date: _____

_____

_____

_____

Date: _____

_____

_____

_____

All the reasons I'm happily divorced

Date: _____

_____

_____

_____

Date: _____

_____

_____

_____

Date: _____

_____

_____

_____

Date: _____

_____

_____

_____

All the reasons I'm happily divorced

Date: _____

_____

_____

_____

Date: _____

_____

_____

_____

Date: _____

_____

_____

_____

Date: _____

_____

_____

_____

All the reasons I'm happily divorced

Date: _____

_____

_____

_____

Date: _____

_____

_____

_____

Date: _____

_____

_____

_____

Date: _____

_____

_____

_____

All the reasons I'm happily divorced

Date: _____

_____

_____

_____

Date: _____

_____

_____

_____

Date: _____

_____

_____

_____

Date: _____

_____

_____

_____

All the reasons I'm happily divorced

Date: _____

_____

_____

_____

Date: _____

_____

_____

_____

Date: _____

_____

_____

_____

Date: _____

_____

_____

_____

All the reasons I'm happily divorced

Date: _____

_____

_____

_____

Date: _____

_____

_____

_____

Date: _____

_____

_____

_____

Date: _____

_____

_____

_____

All the reasons I'm happily divorced

Date: _____

_____

_____

_____

Date: _____

_____

_____

_____

Date: _____

_____

_____

_____

Date: _____

_____

_____

_____

All the reasons I'm happily divorced

Date: _____

_____

_____

_____

Date: _____

_____

_____

_____

Date: _____

_____

_____

_____

Date: _____

_____

_____

_____

All the reasons I'm happily divorced

Date: _____

_____

_____

_____

Date: _____

_____

_____

_____

Date: _____

_____

_____

_____

Date: _____

_____

_____

_____

All the reasons I'm happily divorced

Date: _____

_____

_____

_____

Date: _____

_____

_____

_____

Date: _____

_____

_____

_____

Date: _____

_____

_____

_____

All the reasons I'm happily divorced

Date: _____

_____

_____

_____

Date: _____

_____

_____

_____

Date: _____

_____

_____

_____

Date: _____

_____

_____

_____

All the reasons I'm happily divorced

Date: _____

_____

_____

_____

Date: _____

_____

_____

_____

Date: _____

_____

_____

_____

Date: _____

_____

_____

_____

All the reasons I'm happily divorced

Date: _____

_____

_____

_____

Date: _____

_____

_____

_____

Date: _____

_____

_____

_____

Date: _____

_____

_____

_____

All the reasons I'm happily divorced

Date: _____

_____

_____

_____

Date: _____

_____

_____

_____

Date: _____

_____

_____

_____

Date: _____

_____

_____

_____

All the reasons I'm happily divorced

Date: _____

_____

_____

_____

Date: _____

_____

_____

_____

Date: _____

_____

_____

_____

Date: _____

_____

_____

_____

All the reasons I'm happily divorced

Date: _____

_____
_____
_____

Date: _____

_____
_____
_____

Date: _____

_____
_____
_____

Date: _____

_____
_____
_____

All the reasons I'm happily divorced

Date: _____

_____

_____

_____

Date: _____

_____

_____

_____

Date: _____

_____

_____

_____

Date: _____

_____

_____

_____

All the reasons I'm happily divorced

Date: _____

_____

_____

_____

Date: _____

_____

_____

_____

Date: _____

_____

_____

_____

Date: _____

_____

_____

_____

All the reasons I'm happily divorced

Date: _____

_____

_____

_____

Date: _____

_____

_____

_____

Date: _____

_____

_____

_____

Date: _____

_____

_____

_____

All the reasons I'm happily divorced

Date: _____

_____

_____

_____

Date: _____

_____

_____

_____

Date: _____

_____

_____

_____

Date: _____

_____

_____

_____

All the reasons I'm happily divorced

Date: _____

_____

_____

_____

Date: _____

_____

_____

_____

Date: _____

_____

_____

_____

Date: _____

_____

_____

_____

All the reasons I'm happily divorced

Date: _____

_____

_____

_____

Date: _____

_____

_____

_____

Date: _____

_____

_____

_____

Date: _____

_____

_____

All the reasons I'm happily divorced

Date: _____

_____

_____

_____

Date: _____

_____

_____

_____

Date: _____

_____

_____

_____

Date: _____

_____

_____

_____

All the reasons I'm happily divorced

Date: _____

_____
_____
_____

Date: _____

_____
_____
_____

Date: _____

_____
_____
_____

Date: _____

_____
_____
_____

All the reasons I'm happily divorced

Date: _____

_____

_____

_____

Date: _____

_____

_____

_____

Date: _____

_____

_____

_____

Date: _____

_____

_____

_____

All the reasons I'm happily divorced

Date: _____

_____

_____

_____

Date: _____

_____

_____

_____

Date: _____

_____

_____

_____

Date: _____

_____

_____

_____

All the reasons I'm happily divorced

Date: _____

_____

_____

_____

Date: _____

_____

_____

_____

Date: _____

_____

_____

_____

Date: _____

_____

_____

_____

All the reasons I'm happily divorced

Date: _____

_____

_____

_____

Date: _____

_____

_____

_____

Date: _____

_____

_____

_____

Date: _____

_____

_____

_____

All the reasons I'm happily divorced

Date: _____

_____

_____

_____

Date: _____

_____

_____

_____

Date: _____

_____

_____

_____

Date: _____

_____

_____

_____

All the reasons I'm happily divorced

Date: _____

_____

_____

_____

Date: _____

_____

_____

_____

Date: _____

_____

_____

_____

Date: _____

_____

_____

_____

All the reasons I'm happily divorced

Date: _____

_____

_____

_____

Date: _____

_____

_____

_____

Date: _____

_____

_____

_____

Date: _____

_____

_____

_____

All the reasons I'm happily divorced

Date: _____

_____

_____

_____

Date: _____

_____

_____

_____

Date: _____

_____

_____

_____

Date: _____

_____

_____

_____

All the reasons I'm happily divorced

Date: _____

_____

_____

_____

Date: _____

_____

_____

_____

Date: _____

_____

_____

_____

Date: _____

_____

_____

_____

All the reasons I'm happily divorced

Date: _____

_____

_____

_____

Date: _____

_____

_____

_____

Date: _____

_____

_____

_____

Date: _____

_____

_____

_____

All the reasons I'm happily divorced

Date: _____

_____

_____

_____

Date: _____

_____

_____

_____

Date: _____

_____

_____

_____

Date: _____

_____

_____

_____

All the reasons I'm happily divorced

Date: _____

_____

_____

_____

Date: _____

_____

_____

_____

Date: _____

_____

_____

_____

Date: _____

_____

_____

_____

All the reasons I'm happily divorced

Date: _____

_____

_____

_____

Date: _____

_____

_____

_____

Date: _____

_____

_____

_____

Date: _____

_____

_____

_____

All the reasons I'm happily divorced

Date: _____

_____

_____

_____

Date: _____

_____

_____

_____

Date: _____

_____

_____

_____

Date: _____

_____

_____

_____

All the reasons I'm happily divorced

Date: _____

_____

_____

_____

Date: _____

_____

_____

_____

Date: _____

_____

_____

_____

Date: _____

_____

_____

_____

All the reasons I'm happily divorced

Date: _____

_____

_____

_____

Date: _____

_____

_____

_____

Date: _____

_____

_____

_____

Date: _____

_____

_____

_____

All the reasons I'm happily divorced

Date: _____

_____

_____

_____

Date: _____

_____

_____

_____

Date: _____

_____

_____

_____

Date: _____

_____

_____

_____

All the reasons I'm happily divorced

Date: _____

_____

_____

_____

Date: _____

_____

_____

_____

Date: _____

_____

_____

_____

Date: _____

_____

_____

_____

All the reasons I'm happily divorced

Date: _____

_____

_____

_____

Date: _____

_____

_____

_____

Date: _____

_____

_____

_____

Date: _____

_____

_____

_____

All the reasons I'm happily divorced

Date: _____

_____

_____

_____

Date: _____

_____

_____

_____

Date: _____

_____

_____

_____

Date: _____

_____

_____

_____

All the reasons I'm happily divorced

Date: _____

_____

_____

_____

Date: _____

_____

_____

_____

Date: _____

_____

_____

_____

Date: _____

_____

_____

_____

All the reasons I'm happily divorced

Date: _____

_____

_____

_____

Date: _____

_____

_____

_____

Date: _____

_____

_____

_____

Date: _____

_____

_____

_____

All the reasons I'm happily divorced

Date: _____

_____

_____

_____

Date: _____

_____

_____

_____

Date: _____

_____

_____

_____

Date: _____

_____

_____

_____

All the reasons I'm happily divorced

Date: _____

_____

_____

_____

Date: _____

_____

_____

_____

Date: _____

_____

_____

_____

Date: _____

_____

_____

_____

All the reasons I'm happily divorced

Date: _____

_____

_____

_____

Date: _____

_____

_____

_____

Date: _____

_____

_____

_____

Date: _____

_____

_____

_____

All the reasons I'm happily divorced

Date: _____

_____

_____

_____

Date: _____

_____

_____

_____

Date: _____

_____

_____

_____

Date: _____

_____

_____

_____

Made in the USA
Las Vegas, NV
22 October 2024

10284836R10057